Analyze This: Testing Materials

by Kelli Hicks

Science Content Editor:
Shirley Duke

rourkeeducationalmedia.com

Teacher Notes available at
rem4teachers.com

Science Content Editor: Shirley Duke holds a bachelor's degree in biology and a master's degree in education from Austin College in Sherman, Texas. She taught science in Texas at all levels for twenty-five years before starting to write for children. Her science books include *You Can't Wear These Genes, Infections, Infestations, and Diseases, Enterprise STEM, Forces and Motion at Work, Environmental Disasters,* and *Gases.* She continues writing science books and also works as a science content editor.

www.rourkeeducationalmedia.com

Photo credits: Cover © Andrey Armyagov;Pages 2/3 © Rigamondis; Pages 4/5 © cubephoto; Pages 6/7 © Monika Wisniewska, Dani Vincek; Pages 8/9 © Brian A Jackson, Africa Studio, Tatik22, igor.stevanovic, mikeledray, Monkey Business Images; Pages 10/11 © Christian Lopetz, Viktor88, Joe Belanger; Pages 12/13 © Christian Lopetz; Pages 14/15 © gudak, Alhovik; Pages 16/17 © Denis Vrublevski, artiomp; Pages 18/19 © Bandy, Subbotina Anna, Tarasyuk Igor; Pages 20/21 © R.legosyn, Aaron Amat

Editor: Jeanne Sturm

My Science Library series produced by Nicola Stratford Designs, Florida for Rourke Educational Media.

Library of Congress PCN Data

Hicks, Kelli
 Analyze This: Testing Materials / Kelli Hicks.
    p. cm. -- (My Science Library)
 ISBN 978-1-61810-110-5 (Hard cover) (alk. paper)
 ISBN 978-1-61810-243-0 (Soft cover)
 Library of Congress Control Number: 2012930308

Rourke Educational Media
Printed in the United States of America,
North Mankato, Minnesota

rourkeeducationalmedia.com

customerservice@rourkeeducationalmedia.com
PO Box 643328 Vero Beach, Florida 32964

Table of Contents

Conducting Tests

Water collects in a puddle and then seems to disappear as the day goes on. Where did the water go? How can you find out? By observing, experimenting, measuring, and testing materials, scientists find out about how the world works. They try to answer questions that might lead to new discoveries.

Did You Know?

Not all sources provide safe drinking water. Scientists test water samples for bacteria, viruses, or various minerals that could make people sick. By analyzing the contents, researchers have developed ways of cleaning up contaminated water to make it safe for people to drink.

A scientist tests polluted water to determine the effect of the pollutants on the animals that live there.

When beginning an investigation, scientists follow specific steps called the scientific method. First, scientists ask a question. They research their topic and develop a **hypothesis**, a smart guess about what the result of the investigation might be. Then, they test the hypothesis by conducting an experiment. They collect data, analyze it, and use their findings to prove or change their original hypothesis. They use their new knowledge to test other ideas.

The Scientific Method

1. Ask a question.
2. Observe. Research what's already known.
3. Form a new idea to test.
4. Test the idea with an experiment that can be repeated by others.
5. Draw a conclusion.
6. Report the results.

If an idea doesn't work out, start again at step 3!

How long does it take for mold to grow on a piece of bread?

1. Rub a cotton swab on the ground and then roll the swab across a piece of bread.
2. Add a few drops of water and seal the bread in a plastic bag.
3. Watch and record the data.

What did you find out? Remember to be safe. Leave the bread inside the sealed bag and throw it away when your experiment is finished.

Mold may look green like a plant, but it is actually a fungus.

What is Matter?

●○●○●○●○●○●○●○●○●○●○●○●○

What have scientists learned from years of testing and research? They have discovered that all objects on Earth are made of **matter**. Matter is anything that has mass and takes up space. The most common forms of matter are solid, liquid, and gas. Physical changes such as motion, temperature, or **pressure** can cause a change in the form, or state, of matter.

solid

liquid

gas

You cannot see the shape of a gas, but you can see how much space it takes up. The size of the balloons shows how much air is inside them.

Freezing will change most liquids into solids. Heating will melt some solids into liquids.

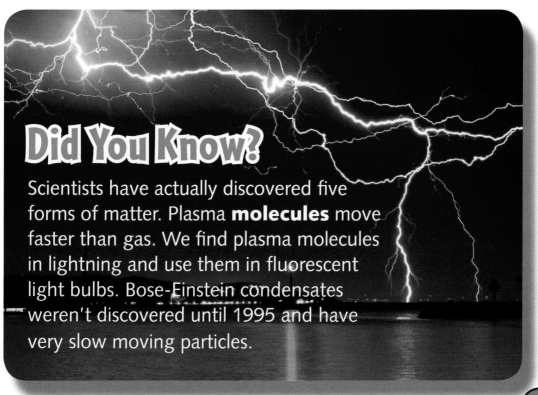

Did You Know?

Scientists have actually discovered five forms of matter. Plasma **molecules** move faster than gas. We find plasma molecules in lightning and use them in fluorescent light bulbs. Bose-Einstein condensates weren't discovered until 1995 and have very slow moving particles.

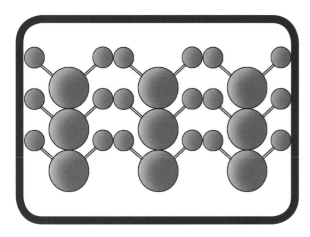

molecules in a solid

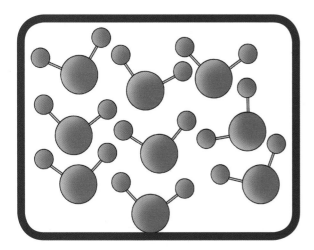

molecules in a liquid

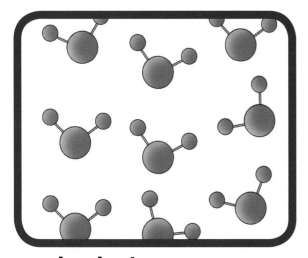

molecules in a gas

The molecules in a solid are tightly packed together. They vibrate, but their movement is limited. A solid keeps its shape. A liquid has size and **volume**, but it doesn't have its own shape. The particles have more space between one another so the particles in a liquid are able to move around more than those in a solid. In order to turn the liquid into a solid, you have to slow down the movement of the particles. Gas particles move freely and have no shape.

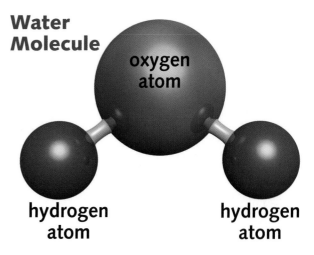

Water Molecule

oxygen atom

hydrogen atom

hydrogen atom

Molecules form when two or more atoms bond. All the matter around us, both natural and man-made, is made up of atoms.

TEST THIS

How can you change water into a gas?

Pour water into an ice cube tray. Put the tray into the freezer. Water freezes at zero degrees Fahrenheit (32 degrees Celsius). If you want to turn the water into a gas, you need to allow the particles to move more quickly. With help from an adult, boil water at 212 degrees Fahrenheit (100 degrees Celsius) and you will see steam forming above the pan. The liquid changed into a gas and vaporized into the air.

Always be safe when using heat or chemicals in an experiment.

Elements and the Periodic Table

Elements are the building blocks of all matter. Scientists use the periodic table to organize the elements. Scientists have found more than 100 elements. Gaps in the early periodic table were filled in as elements were discovered. They put them into the chart based on their structure, characteristics, and properties.

Analyze This

Look at the periodic table. Make a chart with two columns. In the first column, list the elements that you already know. In the second column, list elements you want to investigate further. Be a scientist and research an element. Share your findings with a friend.

Period	Group 1	2	3	4	5
1	1 **H** 1.008				
2	3 **Li** 6.941	4 **Be** 9.012			
3	11 **Na** 22.99	12 **Mg** 24.31			
4	19 **K** 39.10	20 **Ca** 40.08	21 **Sc** 44.96	22 **Ti** 47.88	23 **V** 50.94
5	37 **Rb** 85.47	38 **Sr** 87.62	39 **Y** 88.91	40 **Zr** 91.22	41 **Nb** 92.91
6	55 **Cs** 132.9	56 **Ba** 137.3	*	72 **Hf** 178.5	73 **Ta** 180.9
7	87 **Fr** (223)	88 **Ra** (226)	**	104 **Rf** (261)	105 **Db** (262)

*Lanthanide Series

57 **La** 138.9	58 **Ce** 140.1

**Actinide Series

89 **Ac** (227)	90 **Th** 232

12

						18
						2 **He** 4.003

13	**14**	**15**	**16**	**17**	
5 **B** 10.81	6 **C** 12.01	7 **N** 14.01	8 **O** 16.00	9 **F** 19.00	10 **Ne** 20.18
13 **Al** 26.98	14 **Si** 28.09	15 **P** 30.97	16 **S** 32.07	17 **Cl** 35.45	18 **Ar** 39.95

6	**7**	**8**	**9**	**10**	**11**	**12**						
24 **Cr** 52.00	25 **Mn** 54.94	26 **Fe** 55.85	27 **Co** 58.93	28 **Ni** 58.69	29 **Cu** 63.55	30 **Zn** 65.39	31 **Ga** 69.72	32 **Ge** 72.64	33 **As** 74.92	34 **Se** 78.96	35 **Br** 79.90	36 **Kr** 83.79
42 **Mo** 95.94	43 **Tc** (98)	44 **Ru** 101.1	45 **Rh** 102.9	46 **Pd** 106.4	47 **Ag** 107.9	48 **Cd** 112.4	49 **In** 114.8	50 **Sn** 118.7	51 **Sb** 121.8	52 **Te** 127.6	53 **I** 126.9	54 **Xe** 131.3
74 **W** 183.9	75 **Re** 186.2	76 **Os** 190.2	77 **Ir** 192.2	78 **Pt** 195.1	79 **Au** 197.0	80 **Hg** 200.5	81 **Tl** 204.4	82 **Pb** 207.2	83 **Bi** 209.0	84 **Po** (209)	85 **At** (210)	86 **Rn** (222)
106 **Sg** (266)	107 **Bh** (264)	108 **Hs** (277)	109 **Mt** (268)	110 **Ds** (281)	111 **Rg** (272)	112 **Cn** (285)	113 **Uut** (286)	114 **Fl** (289)	115 **Uup** (289)	116 **Lv** (291)	117 **Uus** (294)	118 **Uuo** (294)

59 **Pr** 140.9	60 **Nd** 144.2	61 **Pm** (145)	62 **Sm** 150.4	63 **Eu** 152.0	64 **Gd** 157.2	65 **Tb** 158.9	66 **Dy** 162.5	67 **Ho** 164.9	68 **Er** 167.3	69 **Tm** 168.9	70 **Yb** 173.0	71 **Lu** 175.0
91 **Pa** 231	92 **U** 238	93 **Np** (237)	94 **Pu** (244)	95 **Am** (243)	96 **Cm** (247)	97 **Bk** (247)	98 **Cf** (251)	99 **Es** (252)	100 **Fm** (257)	101 **Md** (258)	102 **No** (259)	103 **Lr** (262)

Over 75 percent of the elements in the periodic table are metals. How do you know if something is a metal? Metals are good at conducting electricity. They tend to be shiny and **malleable**, meaning that their shape can be changed. They also combine with other elements easily. Silver (Ag), gold (Au), and potassium (K) are all examples of metals.

A blacksmith heats up metal in a fire, then uses a hammer to shape the metal.

Analyze This

Have you ever used a thermometer? As the temperature increases, what do you notice about the liquid inside the thermometer? What would happen if the temperature dropped? Mercury (Hg) is a liquid metal that is often used in a thermometer. When the liquid metal is heated, the metal expands, which causes it to rise.

Look at the two thermometers. Which one shows a summer temperature?

Phosphorus (P) and carbon (C) are solid non-metals. They do not conduct heat or electricity well, and they tend to be brittle and dull. Non-metals do not reflect light.

Did You Know?

A diamond is a type of carbon, a non-metal.

The last group of elements is metalloids. They share properties of both metals and non-metals. Many are brittle like non-metals, but resemble metals in shine or luster. Some of the metalloids can conduct electricity when exposed to high temperatures. Boron (B) and silicon (Si) are metalloids.

Silicon makes up about 28 percent of the Earth's crust.

How can you test malleability to find out if an element is a metal or non-metal?

If you hammer the object and the shape changes, it is a metal. If it shatters or breaks apart it is not a metal. What happens if you hammer an object made of steel? What about a piece of sulfur?

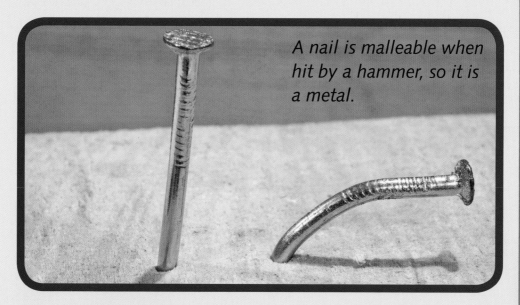

A nail is malleable when hit by a hammer, so it is a metal.

Is sulfur a metal? It looks like a metal, but it shatters when you hammer it.

Mixtures, Solutions, and Compounds

Many things that exist in the world are **mixtures**. Mixtures are physical combinations of matter that can be separated. Sand is a mixture. It has different particles that can be separated from each other, but the physical composition does not change.

A bowl of cereal is a mixture. The two parts share the same bowl, but you can see that the cereal and the milk are still separate.

A solution is a type of mixture. When you combine two things, they mix and spread out evenly. A solution can be made of two liquids, like bleach and water. Or it can be a solid and a liquid. Salt stirred into water makes a solution. The salt is a **solute**. It is the part of the solution that **dissolves**. The water is called the solvent. It is the part that dissolves the other substance. All solutions are mixtures. However, not all mixtures are solutions.

Instant coffee is a solution. The coffee is the solute, and the water is the solvent.

When you mix colored crystals and sugar with water, you create a solution known as Kool-Aid.

Sweet water:

1. Fill two glasses with warm water.
2. Add 2 tablespoons of sugar to one glass and 2 tablespoons of corn starch to the other and mix.

Look at the water in each glass. Is it clear? Next, use a paper funnel and pour the sugar water through the funnel into a plastic bottle. What do you see? Did you collect any sugar?

Now try the corn starch. The corn starch forms a **suspension** in the liquid. It will settle out if left for a time. It doesn't mix well with the water and will separate from it when poured through the filter.

Did You Know?

Pancake mix is a suspension because it is a fluid having small bits of flour floating in it.

TEST THIS

Pudding:

Follow the directions on the box to make instant pudding. What happens when the powder mixes with the milk? The water in the mix makes the pudding thicken and form a **colloid**. The matter in a colloid is spread evenly throughout the mixture and will stay there. The particles won't settle to the bottom of the bowl.

When two or more elements combine, a compound forms. The original elements lose their characteristics and become something completely new. A physical force cannot change a compound. When naming compounds, scientists use the name of the metal first, and then add –ide to the second element.

Scientists analyze mixtures, solutions, and compounds to understand how materials work. You can think like a scientist, too. What questions do you want to answer?

How will you experiment and analyze your results?

Did You Know?

When sodium (Na) and chlorine (Cl) combine chemically, they become sodium chloride (NaCl), or table salt.

Show What You Know

1. Describe the states of matter.

2. Compare and contrast a mixture and a compound.

3. What are elements? Why are they important?

Glossary

colloid (KAH-loid): a solution where the particles remain suspended

dissolves (di-SOLVZ): seems to disappear when mixed with a liquid

elements (EL-uh-muhntz): the basic parts of matter; they cannot be split into simpler substances

hypothesis (hye-POTH-uh-sis): temporary prediction that can be tested about how a scientific investigation will turn out

malleable (MAL-ee-uh-buhl): easily molded into a different shape

matter (MAT-ur): anything that has mass and takes up space

mixtures (MIKS-churz): consisting of different substances or elements combined together

molecules (MOL-uh-kyoolz): the smallest parts of a substance that display the chemical properties of that substance

pressure (PRESH-ur): the force produced by pushing on something

solute (SAHL-yoot): the substance that dissolves in a liquid

suspension (suh-SPEN-shuhn): a mixture of visible particles that will settle to the bottom of the container

volume (VOL-yuhm): the amount of space a liquid occupies

Index

Websites to Visit

www.chem4kids.com

www.kids-science-experiments.com

www.fossweb.com

About the Author

Kelli Hicks loves to read, write, and explore science. She lives in Tampa with her two children, Mackenzie and Barrett, her husband, and her golden retriever, Gingerbread.

Ask The Author!
www.rem4students.com

24